THE OFFICIAL
UEFA euro 96

Superstars

UEFA
euro
96
England ©

Keir Radnedge
Editor of *World Soccer* magazine

THIS IS A CARLTON BOOK

This edition published 1996
by Carlton Books, 20 St Anne's Court,
Wardour Street, London W1V 3AW

Text and design copyright © 1996 Carlton Books Limited

© The EURO 96™ emblem is a Copyright and Trademark of UEFA
The official EURO 96™ Mascot © 1994 ISL TM

ISBN 0 75251 825 9

Printed in Italy

PICTURE ACKNOWLEDGEMENTS
The publishers would like to thank the following sources for their
permission to reproduce the photographs in this book:
Allsport/Shaun Botterill, Clive Brunskill, Simon Bruty, David
Cannon, Chris Cole, Mike Hewitt, Gary M Prior, Ben Radford,
Vandystadt; Colorsport; Popperfoto/SAG, Joyner, Bob Thomas.

(Opposite) **Hallowed turf:** Wembley Stadium will stage the
Final of the 1996 European Championship on Sunday, 30 June.

Introduction

Every manager says it: "The game is all about players." In the case of EURO 96™ — the finals of the European Championship — what players indeed!

The most outstanding talents from the Continent at the heart of the world game are bringing to England their ambitions and skills, offering great saves and great goals.

The history of the European Championship is a Who's Who of football. In the beginning there was Lev Yashin, the great Soviet goalkeeper, in 1960. Then came Spain's Luis Suarez, Italy's Sandro Mazzola and Luigi Riva, West Germany's Franz Beckenbauer and Gerd Müller, French genius Michel Platini and Holland's Ruud Gullit and Marco Van Basten. Four years ago, the rank outsiders from Denmark came from nowhere to seize the title and turn the likes of Peter Schmeichel and Brian Laudrup into international superstars overnight. Such a crowning glory may await the heroes embarking upon the challenge of EURO 96™.

Will it be experienced campaigners such as Italy's Roberto Baggio, Germany's Jürgen Klinsmann or Holland's Dennis Bergkamp? Perhaps a firebrand forward such as England's Paul Gascoigne, Frenchman Eric Cantona or Bulgaria's Hristo Stoichkov? Or maybe one of the glittering newcomers to the big stage such as Italy's Alessandro Del Piero, Portugal's Paulo Sousa or Holland's Patrick Kluivert?

England, as hosts, will not fear any of the continental challengers. Thirty years ago, England, also as hosts, defeated the best of the rest to win the World Cup. In terms of the worldwide TV audience, of the cash on offer and of the glory available, EURO 96™ is the biggest sporting event England has ever staged.

Such knowledge will surely inspire David Seaman, Tony Adams, Alan Shearer and their team-mates. Nothing in their careers could compare with the chance to become football legends — as a team and as individuals.

Contents

Tony Adams 4

Roberto Baggio 5

Dennis Bergkamp . . . 6

Zvonimir Boban 7

Eric Cantona 8

John Collins 9

Alex Del Piero 10

Paul Gascoigne 11

Gheorghe Hagi 12

Hakan Sukur 13

Thomas Hässler 14

Marc Hottiger 15

Andrei Kanchelskis . 16

Jürgen Klinsmann . 17

Patrick Kluivert 18

Brian Laudrup 19

Paolo Maldini 20

Ally McCoist 21

Paul McStay 22

David Platt 23

Peter Schmeichel . . . 24

David Seaman 25

Alan Shearer 26

Tomas Skuhravy . . . 27

Paulo Sousa 28

Hristo Stoichkov . . . 29

Davor Suker 30

Gianfranco Zola . . . 31

Andoni Zubizarreta . 32

UEFA **euro 96** *England* ©

Tony Adams

BORN: London,
10 October 1966

CLUB: Arsenal

POSITION/STYLE OF PLAY:
Central defender/solid on
the ground and dominant
in the air

INTERNATIONAL CAREER:
Debut vs. Spain, 1987
(38 appearances, 4 goals)

MOST LIKELY TO:
Frighten the opposing attack
into submission

LEAST LIKELY TO:
Take any risks

Tony Adams may be nicknamed "Donkey" by fans of Arsenal's rivals, but the truth of the matter is that they envy the power and commanding presence he provides at the centre of the Gunners' defence. Ever since his first-team debut, in a 2–1 defeat by Sunderland in November 1983, Adams has been an inspiration. Even now, at 29, he has lifted more silverware than any skipper in Arsenal's history, after becoming one of the club's youngest captains in March 1988. Adams was at the heart of all Arsenal's successes under the managership of George Graham. His great leadership run began with Arsenal's 2–1 win over Liverpool in the Littlewoods-sponsored League Cup Final of 1987. He led Arsenal to the most dramatic League Championship ever, in 1989 – snatching the prize away from champions-elect Liverpool at Anfield, the winning goal coming with almost the last kick of the final game – and a second title in 1991. In 1993 came the FA Cup as well as the League Cup – now backed by Coca-Cola. Adams then led Arsenal successfully into Europe as they triumphed over Italians Parma in the 1994 Cup-winners Cup Final in Copenhagen. All the time, Adams was enhancing his reputation at the heart of England's defence. He made his debut for his country against Spain nine years ago and has been virtually ever-present under the managership of Terry Venables.

England

Roberto Baggio

Goals, grace and great gifts have marked out Roberto Baggio ever since he was a teenager. Now Milan's superstar awaits the national team triumph to crown a great career. Baggio's hero-worshippers call him *Il Codino Divino* – the Divine Ponytail – for this is a player and a man for whom style is second nature. Fiorentina were the first Serie A club whose squad he enriched. His world record £8 million transfer to Juventus, in the summer of 1990, caused Fiorentina fans to lay siege to the club offices for three days and the riot police were called out to protect directors. A few weeks later, Baggio demonstrated, in the World Cup finals, just why he was worth so much, in particular with one wonderful solo goal against the Czechs. Juventus loved him as much as the Florentines. At USA '94, Baggio's goals lifted Italy to victories over Nigeria, Spain and Bulgaria. In the semi-final victory over Bulgaria, however, Baggio strained a hamstring, and he was not really fit for the Final against Brazil. Baggio's miss in the penalty shoot-out offered Brazil their victory. But no one blamed him. If it had not been for Baggio, Italy would not have been in the Final. Baggio bounced back the next season to lead Juventus to the Italian league title before moving to Milan – and setting his sights on new glory with Italy.

BORN: Caldogno, 18 February 1967
CLUBS: Vicenza, Fiorentina, Juventus, Milan
POSITION/STYLE OF PLAY: Forward/likes to turn up anywhere in attack
INTERNATIONAL CAREER: Debut vs. Holland, 1988 (44 appearances, 24 goals)
MOST LIKELY TO: Dart through a massed defence and score the decisive goal
LEAST LIKELY TO: Appreciate being substituted

Italy

UEFA euro 96 England

Dennis Bergkamp

BORN: Amsterdam, 18 May 1969
CLUBS: Ajax Amsterdam,
   Internazionale (Italy),
   Arsenal (England)
POSITION/STYLE:
   Striker/prefers to lurk just
   behind the target man
INTERNATIONAL CAREER:
   Debut vs. Italy, 1990
   (41 appearances, 23 goals)
MOST LIKELY TO: Give all the
   credit for his own achievements
   to his team-mates
LEAST LIKELY TO:
   Say he loves Italian football

Italian fans had mixed feelings about seeing Dennis Bergkamp leave Internazionale when he joined Arsenal in 1995. On the one hand they appreciated the vision, touch and control of the player named Dennis after his father's favourite player – Denis Law. However, they had been misled into expecting a Dutch goal machine in the manner of Marco Van Basten, of neighbours Milan. Bergkamp had, indeed, succeeded injury-embattled Van Basten as attacking spearhead with Ajax. But the two players could not be compared. Van Basten roamed the width of the attacking line waiting for the ball; Bergkamp preferred to drop deep himself, searching for space and an opportunity to help guide the attack. Not for Bergkamp the lone striker's role. He prefers to shadow the target man, then pounce to devastating effect – as he did, for example, in the 1994 World Cup against England in the qualifying competition in Rotterdam and, then again, against the Republic of Ireland in Orlando in the finals. Moving to Arsenal offered Bergkamp the chance to rebuild his confidence just in time to threaten his hosts' bid for EURO 96™ glory. Then he can fulfil the brilliance which so impressed Ajax in his teenage days that he was once flown out to Sweden on the day of a Cup-winners Cup tie against Malmo – because he had been sitting a school exam the previous day when the rest of the squad travelled.

UEFA EURO 96 England

Holland

Zvonimir Boban

The name of Zvonimir Boban was first whispered down the international grapevine back in 1987. He was already such a complete footballer, with remarkable physical presence for one so young, that he was soon playing for the former Yugoslavia's full national team. Tragic history has, since those heady days, scarred the country and its people. As the civil strife began so Boban transferred away from Dinamo (now FC Croatia) of Zagreb to Italy. He spent one adjustment season in the south-east, with Bari, before joining Milan, but it took time before he succeeded in imposing himself as one of the regular foreign players in the side. The initial problem was Serie A's limit of three foreign players in any one match, and Milan had six imports, including Dutchmen Frank Rijkaard, Marco Van Basten and Ruud Gullit. Coach Fabio Capello, however, recognized Boban had the talent to replace either Gullit or Rijkaard and, despite infrequent early appearances, Boban quickly became a crowd favourite thanks to his dangerous free kicks. Capello then gave Boban a regular first-team opportunity and he was outstanding in the 4–0 victory over Barcelona in the 1994 Champions Cup Final. Now, with Croatia established as an independent state, Boban can make up for the chance lost when Yugoslavia were barred from the finals of four years ago.

BORN: Imotski, 8 October 1968
CLUBS: Dinamo Zagreb (Yugoslavia), Bari (Italy), Milan (Italy)
POSITION/STYLE OF PLAY: Midfielder/roams wide down the wings slicing opposing defences wide open
INTERNATIONAL CAREER: Yugoslavia debut vs. Republic of Ireland, 1988; Croatia debut vs. Romania, 1990
MOST LIKELY TO: Dribble round four defenders in the six-yard box — then offer the shooting chance to someone else
LEAST LIKELY TO: Waste a chance of shooting at a free kick

Croatia

Eric Cantona

Manchester United's extravagant exhibitionist is the most gifted and temperamental French player of his generation. He is also one of the most mystifying — as he proved, in the wake of his infamous kung-fu asssault at Selhurst Park, by telling the media: "When seagulls follow the trawler, then it is because they think sardines will be thrown into the sea." Cantona was, at the time, heading into a seven-month suspension imposed by the FA and a community service sentence imposed by the court. But anyone who thought that would be the end of him could not have been more wrong. All the old talent shone as brightly on his triumphant return to action in a 2–2 draw against Liverpool on 1 October 1995. Cantona made United's first goal for Ryan Giggs, then scored their second with a typically nerveless penalty. Cantona has had a number of well-publicized brushes with the French football authorities, too. His international career had already been put on hold as manager Aime Jacquet did not rush to recall his wayward star. All this means that Cantona is by no means certain of a place in the French squad for the forthcoming tournament in his adopted homeland. Thus Cantona needs one more step to complete his rehabilitation — a key role with France at EURO 96™.

BORN: Paris, 24 May 1966
CLUBS: Auxerre, Martigues, Auxerre, Marseille, Bordeaux, Montpellier, Marseille, Nimes, Leeds United (England), Manchester United (England)
POSITION/STYLE OF PLAY: Old-fashioned inside-forward/available to turn defence into attack and the attacks into goals
INTERNATIONAL CAREER: Debut vs. West Germany, 1987 (45 app., 19 goals)
MOST LIKELY TO: Throw sardines at the media
LEAST LIKELY TO: Transfer back to Leeds United

France

John Collins

UEFA euro 96 England ©

The shock waves which followed the European Court of Justice's verdict in the case brought by Belgium's Jean-Marc Bosman opened up an intriguing scenario for Celtic's latest hero, John Collins. His contract was due to expire at the end of the 1995–96 season. He was a man in demand. If he opted for England then the buying club would have to pay a fee. If he opted for the continent then he would not cost a penny — and might expect that revolutionary option to be reflected in a more lucrative contract. Then again, Collins is not only a player of football but a lover of the game. More important to him, however, was the prospect of playing for Scotland at the European competitive peak. As Collins told one questioner: "I have to make this third time lucky." In 1990, Collins did not get a look-in as Scotland crashed out of the World Cup finals in Italy. He came home to a transfer, from Hibernian to Celtic, but this did not prove the expected springboard to a secure role for Scotland. Instead, Collins missed selection for the European finals in Sweden after falling out with national coach Andy Roxburgh. Under successor Craig Brown, however, Collins has returned to favour. He was Scotland's top scorer with four goals in the qualifying campaign and believes they can, for the first time, reach at least the quarter-finals of a top tournament.

BORN: Galashiels, 31 January 1968

CLUBS: Hibernian, Celtic

POSITION/STYLE OF PLAY: Attacking midfielder/always takes the direct line towards goal

INTERNATIONAL CAREER: Debut vs. Saudi Arabia, 1988 (29 appearances, 8 goals)

MOST LIKELY TO: Leave four opposing midfielders trailing in his wake

LEAST LIKELY TO: Want Andy Roxburgh back as national coach

Scotland

UEFA EURO 96 England ©

A lex Del Piero is the new golden boy of Italian football – in succession to the likes of Gianni Rivera and his former Juventus team-mate Roberto Baggio. In fact, Del Piero's emergence "allowed" Juventus the luxury of selling Baggio to Milan last summer. Del Piero made his league debut with Padova at 17. One goal in 14 games as an 18-year-old was enough to earn a transfer to Juve in 1993, and he exploded on Serie A with five goals in 11 games, including a hat-trick against Parma. In 1994–95, he helped inspire Juve to victory in the league championship, and continued with five superb goals in the group stage of the following season's Champions League. Inevitably, an award followed as Italy's Young Player of the Year – justifying the single-minded dedication which has marked Del Piero's rise. He says: "Even as a child I was obsessed by the prospect of playing football. Now I can echo what Gianni Rivera once said: 'I'm a happy man because my hobby and my profession are one and the same.'" Frenchman Michel Platini was his boyhood hero. He pulled pictures out of the club's magazine, *Hurra Juventus*, and pinned them to his bedroom wall. Now Del Piero, making his career with Platini's old club, wants to follow his example and inspire his country – of course, in his case Italy – to European Championship success.

BORN: Conegliano, 9 November 1974
CLUBS: Padova, Juventus
POSITION/STYLE OF PLAY: Forward/exquisite control both for passing and shooting
INTERNATIONAL CAREER: Debut vs. Estonia, 1995 (7 appearances, 1 goal)
MOST LIKELY TO: Emerge from EURO 96™ as the world game's new superstar
LEAST LIKELY TO: Leave Juventus at any time in the next 10 years

Italy

Paul Gascoigne

Paul Gascoigne is the player about whom no one can sit on the fence. Either he is the greatest genius English football has produced since Stanley Matthews, or he is his own worst enemy. "Gazza", on the way up the football ladder, mixed his ability with a clown's demeanour, both at Newcastle and then after his £2 million move to Tottenham. At the 1990 World Cup finals, he was one of the most singular individuals on view. Not only did Gazza's approach help his team-mates relax off the pitch, but he also created David Platt's second-round winner against Belgium. His famous tears in the penalty shoot-out defeat by West Germany in the semi-final earned the sympathy of Italian fans and Lazio won the race to seal the £5.5 million deal with Spurs. A self-inflicted knee injury in Spurs' 1991 Cup Final win over Nottingham Forest delayed his transfer for a year. When Gascoigne did move, eventually, his troubles were anything but over. Lazio's fans loved him, but more injuries meant they never saw the "real" Gascoigne for any effective length of time. Coaches tried to build their teams which could function with or without Gascoigne but, after three years, Lazio could wait no longer and, in 1995, Gascoigne returned to British football, his hunger for trophies taking him to Scottish giants Rangers. If his fitness holds up, then Gazza could be England's "secret weapon" at EURO 96™.

BORN: Gateshead, 27 May 1967
CLUBS: Newcastle United, Tottenham Hotspur, Lazio (Italy), Rangers (Scotland)
POSITION/STYLE OF PLAY: Midfielder/inspirational, unpredictable playmaker
INTERNATIONAL CAREER: Debut vs. Denmark, 1988 (32 appearances, 6 goals)
MOST LIKELY TO: Dribble past three defenders, shoot into top corner and burst into tears
LEAST LIKELY TO: Stay out of the headlines for long

England

Gheorghe Hagi

Gheorghe Hagi is still, to his fans, the "Maradona of the Carpathians" – the nickname created when he scored 100 goals in just over 200 first division games in Romania, and was voted 1988 Footballer of the Year. Hagi was twice the league's top scorer before joining Real Madrid for a Romanian record £2 million after the 1990 World Cup. Hagi had been a youth international at 15 and made his senior debut in a 0–0 draw against Norway in Oslo, aged just 18. In Madrid, the fans liked his virtuosity, but the other players complained he did not work hard enough and he was eventually sold to Brescia of Italy. He stayed, despite Brescia's relegation in 1993, and was one of the most outstanding individuals at the 1994 World Cup finals – scoring one remarkable goal with a floating cross-shot in Romania's opening victory over Colombia. After the finals, Hagi was sold to Barcelona, where the other players again considered him too individualistic. Not Romania manager Anghel Iordanescu, however. He considers Hagi the focal point of his European Championship challenge. Romania have never progressed beyond the quarter-finals of a major event. If they are to break with history, then Hagi needs to bring real bite into their attack – before he retires to running a dental practice back in Bucharest!

BORN: Constanta, 5 February 1965
CLUBS: FC Constanta, Sportul Studentesc, Steaua Bucharest, Real Madrid (Spain), Brescia (Italy), Barcelona (Spain)
POSITION/STYLE OF PLAY: Midfield general/demands that all attacks flow through him
INTERNATIONAL CAREER: Debut vs. Norway, 1983 (94 appearances, 27 goals)
MOST LIKELY TO: Curl in a centre from the wing which turns into a shot on goal in mid-flight
LEAST LIKELY TO: Chase back and tackle opposing forwards

Romania

Hakan Sukur

Turkish teams were, for many years, considered to punch less than their weight. Europe's top nations rated the Turks skilled in midfield, a little naïve in defence and powder-puff in attack. Now that's changed — and one of the men deserving high credit is Hakan Sukur, who leads the Turkish assault on EURO 96™. One reason why Turkish football was underrated was the fact that only a handful of their stars had made the grade beyond their own borders. Midfield men Erdal Keser and Ilyas Tufecki were stars in Germany but then, they had been brought up there. Turkish players — and Hakan is a case in point — do not adapt easily to the very different lifestyle they find abroad. Hakan, a tall and lanky centre-forward, promised to break the mould when he was bought in the summer of 1995 by Italian club Torino. His new team-mates, seeing him in pre-season training, forecast great things for Hakan. They were to be disappointed. Quickly he grew homesick. Family problems, off the pitch, did not help. Hakan was Turkey's seven-goal top scorer in the European Championship qualifying campaign, but he could not find the net as consistently for Torino. Galatasaray, having sold him only four months earlier, splashed out £3 million to take him home in November 1995. Now, after finding his football feet again, Hakan is determined that EURO 96™ will see the real Hakan — the new face of Turkish football.

BORN: Bursa, 1 September 1971
CLUBS: Bursaspor, Galatasaray, Torino (Italy), Galatasaray
POSITION/STYLE OF PLAY: Centre-forward/always eager to put central defenders under pressure on the ball
INTERNATIONAL CAREER: Debut vs. Luxembourg, 1992 (23 appearances, 13 goals)
MOST LIKELY TO: Phone home to his folks every day
LEAST LIKELY TO: Want another transfer abroad

Turkey

Thomas Hässler

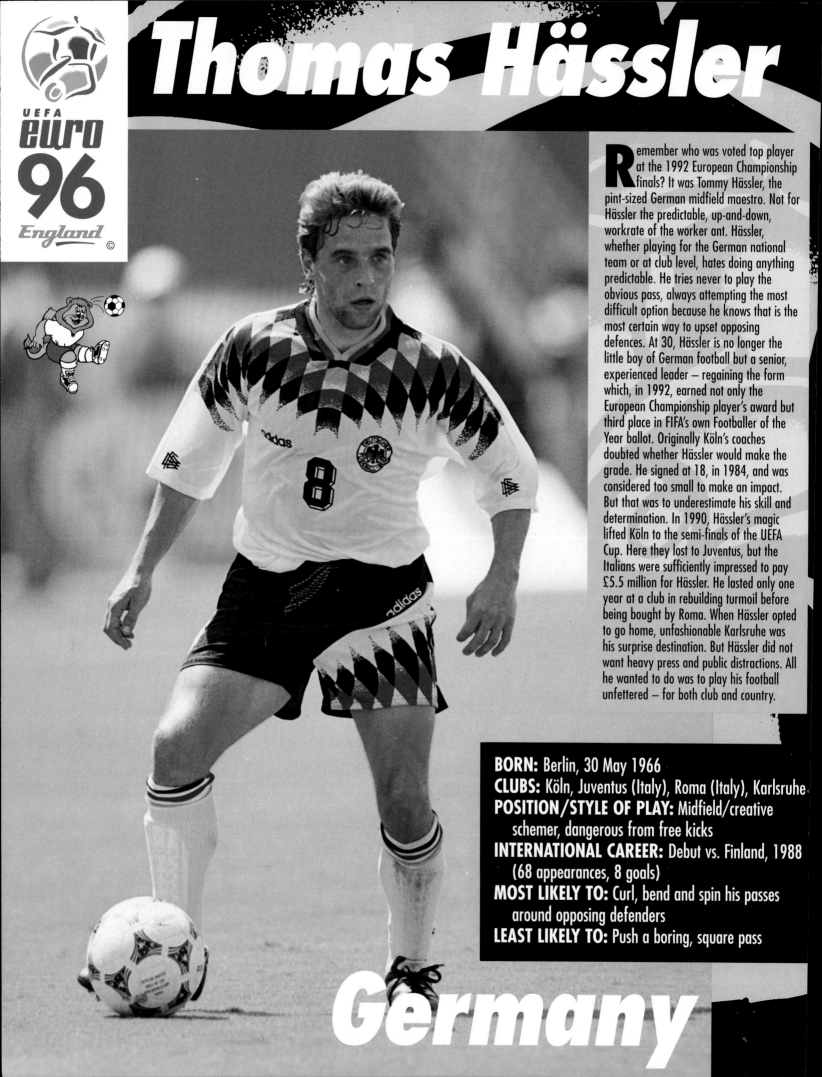

Remember who was voted top player at the 1992 European Championship finals? It was Tommy Hässler, the pint-sized German midfield maestro. Not for Hässler the predictable, up-and-down, workrate of the worker ant. Hässler, whether playing for the German national team or at club level, hates doing anything predictable. He tries never to play the obvious pass, always attempting the most difficult option because he knows that is the most certain way to upset opposing defences. At 30, Hässler is no longer the little boy of German football but a senior, experienced leader – regaining the form which, in 1992, earned not only the European Championship player's award but third place in FIFA's own Footballer of the Year ballot. Originally Köln's coaches doubted whether Hässler would make the grade. He signed at 18, in 1984, and was considered too small to make an impact. But that was to underestimate his skill and determination. In 1990, Hässler's magic lifted Köln to the semi-finals of the UEFA Cup. Here they lost to Juventus, but the Italians were sufficiently impressed to pay £5.5 million for Hässler. He lasted only one year at a club in rebuilding turmoil before being bought by Roma. When Hässler opted to go home, unfashionable Karlsruhe was his surprise destination. But Hässler did not want heavy press and public distractions. All he wanted to do was to play his football unfettered – for both club and country.

BORN: Berlin, 30 May 1966
CLUBS: Köln, Juventus (Italy), Roma (Italy), Karlsruhe
POSITION/STYLE OF PLAY: Midfield/creative schemer, dangerous from free kicks
INTERNATIONAL CAREER: Debut vs. Finland, 1988 (68 appearances, 8 goals)
MOST LIKELY TO: Curl, bend and spin his passes around opposing defenders
LEAST LIKELY TO: Push a boring, square pass

Germany

Marc Hottiger

UEFA euro 96 England ©

Defenders are not usually top of the list when clubs go shopping abroad. So Switzerland's Marc Hottiger is an exception – as well as an exceptional full-back. Kevin Keegan thought so when he paid £800,000 to bring him to England with Newcastle United after the 1994 World Cup finals; then Joe Royle demonstrated similar faith when he paid out a similar sum to sign Hottiger for Everton midway through the 1995–96 season. Hottiger then ran into problems, however, over obtaining a work permit. But the fact that he had long been a renowned international footballer with Switzerland, helped to persuade the British authorities that the entire work permit system, as it applied to foreign players, needed a review. Not that Hottiger had ever been considered a football revolutionary when he launched his career with Renens. Lausanne signed him as a winger in 1988, but an injury crisis forced Hottiger's switch to right-back. His power and pace made him such an instant success that, within a year, he was called up by Switzerland to make his national team debut in a 2–2 draw against Belgium in Basel. National coach Uli Stielike was amazed, saying: "Hottiger is a natural." Hottiger was sold to Sion in 1992, and his attacking capabilities brought him a remarkable seven goals in his first season – form which secured him a place in Switzerland's USA '94 squad.

BORN: Lausanne, 7 November 1967
CLUBS: Renens, Lausanne, Sion, Newcastle United (England), Everton (England)
POSITION/STYLE OF PLAY: Right-back/takes every possible opportunity to raid up the wing
INTERNATIONAL CAREER: Debut vs. Belgium, 1989 (57 appearances, 5 goals)
MOST LIKELY TO: Tackle and dispossess an opposing winger then outrun him
LEAST LIKELY TO: Want to risk applying for another British work permit

Switzerland

Andrei Kanchelskis

Andrei Kanchelskis was once tipped to be one of the richest men in the Ukraine by the time he retires from playing. Everton's flying winger intends to make the most of his talent while he can — and that includes running rings around any full-back who stands in his way at EURO 96™. Ever since arriving in English football from Shakhtyor Donetsk, Kanchelskis has regularly sent flight tickets home so his relatives can visit him. He accepts the uncertain economy of the former Soviet Union means that he must capitalize on his pace and nose for goal. So, why does he play for Russia when Ukraine, his homeland, is now an independent nation in both political and football terms? When the old Soviet Union imploded, its international footballers were offered the option of playing for their "real" countries or for Russia. And, since Russia had won a place in the 1994 World Cup Finals, most opted for Russia. Ironically, Kanchelskis fell out with team manager Pavel Sadyrin and refused to play unless Sadyrin was dismissed. He was not, so Russia went to USA '94 without Kanchelskis — and other top players — and flopped. Kanchelskis took no pleasure in being proved right. He is just glad to have made his peace with new coach Oleg Romantsev. After all, Kanchelskis has inside knowledge of winning trophies in England.

BORN: Donetsk, Ukraine, 23 January 1969

CLUBS: Shakhtyor Donetsk, Manchester United (England), Everton (England)

POSITION/STYLE OF PLAY: Right-winger/dashing attacker with flair, flamboyance and pace

INTERNATIONAL CAREER: USSR debut vs. Poland (37 appearances, 4 goals)

MOST LIKELY TO: Fly in all his family if Russia reach the Final

LEAST LIKELY TO: Want Pavel Sadyrin back as national coach

UEFA euro 96 England ©

Russia

Jürgen Klinsmann

Jürgen Klinsmann cannot wait to return to England for EURO 96™. Germany's outstanding leader — both as captain and in attack — took away fond memories of English fans when he went home from Tottenham Hotspur to Bayern Munich in the summer of 1995. He had played just one season in England but, in that time, charmed every football-lover in the country. It was his self-deprecating humour in responding to criticism that he "dived", it was the example he showed his team-mates in working at his game and it was the goals he scored. It earned him the English Football Writers' Association Footballer of the Year award. Klinsmann exploded as a pro with Stuttgart Kickers. The baker's son then crossed the city to VfB Stuttgart and earned international recognition for the first time in 1987, against Brazil. In 1988, Klinsmann was the German championship's top goalscorer and West Germany's biggest success in the European Championship, both of which helped to earn him the German Footballer of the Year accolade. After leading Stuttgart to the 1989 UEFA Cup Final, he was transferred to Italian giants Internazionale and, a year later, was a major contributor to Germany's World Cup success. After winning the UEFA Cup with Internazionale in 1991, he then tried his luck in France with Monaco, moving to England after USA '94. Whatever the opposition, Klinsmann will surely be the most cosmopolitan player on view at EURO 96™.

BORN: Goppingen, 30 July 1964

CLUBS: Stuttgart Kickers, VfB Stuttgart, Internazionale (Italy), Monaco (France), Tottenham Hotspur (England), Bayern Munich

POSITION/STYLE OF PLAY: Striker/leggy, lanky, awkward, direct, fearless, aggressive

INTERNATIONAL CAREER: Debut vs. Brazil, 1987 (78 appearances, 34 goals)

MOST LIKELY TO: Speak to officials and opponents in their own language

LEAST LIKELY TO: Run the family bakery on retirement

Germany

Patrick Kluivert

Ajax striker Patrick Kluivert became an international sensation overnight, when he appeared as a second-half substitute to score the winner against Milan in last season's Champions League Final. It was by far the most important strike of a season in which he was already established as Ajax's 18-goal top scorer. Kluivert had joined the Ajax youth section from suburban amateur club Schellingwoude. He made his international debut for Holland in an under-15 match against Germany in 1990 – and from that point he was marked for super-stardom. Kluivert made his initial impact with Ajax playing wide on the left in attack. But his height, power and football intelligence meant it was only a matter of time before he was switched inside to more responsible roles. Remarkably, Kluivert played his decisive role in Holland's European qualifying climax despite the trauma caused by his involvement in a fatal car crash. He has had to grow up quickly both off the pitch and on it. As he says: "Which teenager can say he has won the league, the Champions Cup – scoring the winning goal – the World Club Cup ... and that he has then scored both goals in his country's most vital match in years?" No one else fills that bill. Intriguingly, Kluivert believes the best of Holland is yet to come – when they host the finals in four years' time.

BORN: Amsterdam, 1 July 1976
CLUB: Ajax Amsterdam
POSITION/STYLE OF PLAY: Striker/quick and clever, always ready for a one-two which takes him through to a one-on-one with the goalkeeper
INTERNATIONAL CAREER: Debut vs. Czech Republic, 1994 (5 appearances, 1 goal)
MOST LIKELY TO: Score the goal which wins the Final
LEAST LIKELY TO: Spend all his career in Holland

Holland

Brian Laudrup

BORN: Vienna, 22 February 1969
CLUBS: Brondby, Bayer Uerdingen (Germany), Bayern Munich (Germany), Fiorentina (Italy), Milan (Italy), Rangers (Scotland)
POSITION/STYLE OF PLAY: Attacking midfielder/ready to play wide on the wing or in "the hole" to link midfield and attack
INTERNATIONAL CAREER: Debut vs. West Germany, 1987 (60 appearances, 10 goals)
MOST LIKELY TO: Want to play against Scotland in the Final
LEAST LIKELY TO: Be lured back to play in Serie A

Denmark's Brian Laudrup – younger brother of international team-mate Michael – made history, in 1995, when he became the first overseas player to win the Scottish Football Writers' Player of the Year award. The Rangers star collected the accolade less than a year after his move from Italian club Fiorentina, and maintained his club's domination of the prize after Ally McCoist (1992), Andy Goram (1993) and Mark Hateley (1994). Laudrup also made it a foreign double in Britain, since Germany's Jürgen Klinsmann had collected the equivalent award south of the border. It was Laudrup's third player of the year award after the two he collected in Denmark in 1989 and then in the wake of his starring role in his country's sensational European Championship victory of 1992. Laudrup has been described by boss Walter Smith as the signing who made the biggest impact at Ibrox over the past decade. Smith says: "Brian has handled everything so well on and off the park and he is the kind of player which excites the crowd." Laudrup's first move, from the "family" club of Brondby to Bayer Uerdingen in 1989, cost the German club £650,000. Then Bayern Munich paid £2 million for him a year later and Fiorentina a further £3.5 million in 1992. At £2.2 million, it seems that Rangers had a bargain.

Denmark

19

Paolo Maldini

Paolo Maldini, the son of a former captain of Italy and Milan, is not merely one of the world's best defenders — he is universally acknowledged as one of the world's top all-round footballers. He proved the point as Italy finished runners-up at the 1994 World Cup, when his duel with Brazil's Cafu was one of the highlights of the Final. On top of that, Maldini was voted World Player of the Year for 1994 by the magazine *World Soccer*. His claims had long been obvious. Maldini's father, Cesare, is coach to the Italian team which once won the European Under-21 Championship and will contest the Olympic Games crown in Atlanta later this year. Now his son has equalled his father's achievement by winning the European Champions Cup — and emulated his father by playing more than 60 internationals and collecting a World Cup runners-up medal. Maldini, Senior, was, naturally, afforded much of the credit for his son's success. Yet, as Paolo has readily confessed, there were no favours along the way. "If anything," he says, "my father worked me harder than the rest of the Milan youth team, just so no one could accuse him of favouritism." Paolo is taller, leaner and quicker than his father. His reading of the game is equally astute. Now he will captain his country at the European Championship finals — and that's something his father never achieved!

BORN: Milan, 26 June 1968
CLUB: Milan
POSITION/STYLE OF PLAY: Left-back or sweeper/perfect timing in the tackle, great control, pace, accurate shot on overlapping in attack
INTERNATIONAL CAREER: Debut vs. Yugoslavia, 1988 (67 appearances, 4 goals)
MOST LIKELY TO: Raise the Henri Delaunay trophy as winning captain
LEAST LIKELY TO: Allow any winger to get past him

Italy

Ally McCoist

Ally McCoist has been the most prolific goalscorer in Rangers' modern history – with more than 300 goals to his credit – and has twice won the unofficial Golden Boot for the leading league marksman in European football. He would have scored even more goals but for a lengthy absence after he suffered a broken leg, playing for Scotland against Portugal in the 1994 World Cup qualifying competition. McCoist reappeared for Scotland in August 1995, as a substitute in a European Championship qualifier against Greece, and scored the winning goal with virtually his first touch of the ball. That compelling return to international duty earned him the accolade of "football's Peter Pan" from national manager Craig Brown. It also secured serious consideration for McCoist's prospects of returning to play in England – at EURO 96™ – some 13 years after he ended a less-than-satisfying two-year spell in English football. Then, he had scored only eight goals in 56 league games with Sunderland; now, he is the elder statesman of Scottish strikers. As Brown has said: "Ally may well be past 30, but age is no barrier if the player is good enough and determined enough. Look at other veteran players such as England's Peter Beardsley and Ireland's John Aldridge. Ally still loves his football as much as ever. He's still scoring goals like a teenager. Age is no reason why he shouldn't be at the finals."

BORN: Belshill, 24 September 1962
CLUBS: St Johnstone, Sunderland (England), Rangers
POSITION/STYLE OF PLAY: Striker/snapper-up of the merest half-chance
INTERNATIONAL CAREER: Debut vs. Holland, 1986 (49 appearances, 17 goals)
MOST LIKELY TO: Be one of the oldest players at EURO 96™
LEAST LIKELY TO: Be sponsored by a watch and clock manufacturer

Scotland

Paul McStay

Paul McStay is the only member of Scotland's current generation who stands any chance of overtaking Kenny Dalglish's record of 102 international appearances. In the early 1980s, the Celtic midfield general and skipper was a teenage star in the making. Now he is a senior professional – a man whose care for detail is legendary. It even extended, at the European Championship finals in 1992, to having all the windows of his hotel room blacked out so he could take a nap at any time of the day. But then, McStay has a family reputation to defend. Two of his great-uncles captained Celtic and one, Jimmy McStay, went on to become manager during the Second World War. Two brothers were also signed by Celtic and the elder, Willie, played in the first team with Paul. At club level, all McStay's leadership qualities emerged during Celtic's last league and cup double-winning season of 1987–88. At international level, for Scotland, he first made his presence felt by scoring twice at Wembley in a dramatic 5–4 win over England at schoolboy level, in 1980. As a senior, McStay was never better than in the 1992 European finals but, for some reason, his displays did not elicit the expected offers from the continent and he stayed at Parkhead. An ankle injury delayed his start to the 1995–96 season, but McStay was soon back in the thick of the Celtic and Scotland action.

BORN: Hamilton, 22 October 1964
CLUB: Celtic
POSITION/STYLE OF PLAY:
Midfield general/lives up to his nickname of "The Maestro" with his measured passing, organizational control and powerful shot
INTERNATIONAL CAREER:
Debut vs. Uruguay, 1983
(72 appearances, 9 goals)
MOST LIKELY TO: Become Celtic manager himself one day
LEAST LIKELY TO:
Become Rangers manager

Scotland

David Platt

Six years are all it has taken to bring David Platt on the most incredible full soccer circle. In the spring of 1990, he was an up-and-coming, hard-working attacking midfielder, unknown beyond England, and not even particularly well known beyond the immediate confines of Crewe Alexandra (where he started) and Aston Villa (where he had been turned into an international). Then, in the dying seconds of England's World Cup second-round tie against Belgium in Bologna, Platt stole into the six-yard box to volley home a long, penetrating free kick from Paul Gascoigne. England were on their way to the last four and Platt was on his way — to a five-year stretch in Italy. Those years turned Platt from a fresh-faced international apprentice into a suave, stylish, cosmopolitan man of the football world. He joined Bari, learned Italian at high speed and presented the ideal image to charm the media and delight sponsors. Bari was just the start. Despite his efforts Bari went down, but Platt's career went up. Juventus was the next stop, then Sampdoria and a dream attacking partnership with Ruud Gullit. The job of England captain was (Graham) Taylor-made for him. Platt returned to England in the summer of 1995, but a knee injury upset his initial months at Arsenal. At least he was home in time for England's biggest party in 30 years.

England

BORN: Chadderton, 10 June 1966

CLUBS: Crewe Alexandra, Aston Villa, Bari (Italy), Juventus (Italy), Sampdoria (Italy), Arsenal

POSITION/STYLE OF PLAY: Attacking midfielder/always dangerous with his blind-side runs into space in the penalty box

INTERNATIONAL CAREER: Debut vs. Italy, 1989 (55 appearances, 26 goals)

MOST LIKELY TO: Charm the media into taking England's EURO 96™ challenge seriously

LEAST LIKELY TO: Call a foreign journalist a "buffoon"

Peter Schmeichel

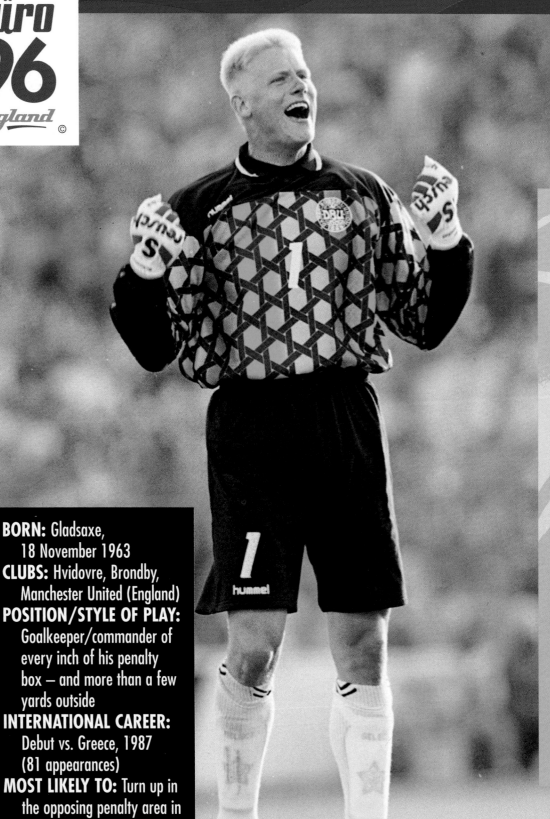

BORN: Gladsaxe,
18 November 1963

CLUBS: Hvidovre, Brondby,
Manchester United (England)

POSITION/STYLE OF PLAY:
Goalkeeper/commander of
every inch of his penalty
box — and more than a few
yards outside

INTERNATIONAL CAREER:
Debut vs. Greece, 1987
(81 appearances)

MOST LIKELY TO: Turn up in
the opposing penalty area in
a crisis

LEAST LIKELY TO: Let a
fellow defender get to the
ball first

Once upon a time, goalkeepers prowled their six-yard box and that was where their influence began and ended. Nowadays, the likes of Danish keeper Peter Schmeichel have turned tradition upside down. The giant Dane proved the point as Manchester United battled against Rotor Volgograd in the UEFA Cup. With the minutes ticking away, Schmeichel strode the length of the pitch and into the Russian penalty box at a corner — and he scored! That goal was not quite enough to save the day for United, but it emphasized the towering influence Schmeichel brings to every side for whom he plays — whether in the league or the European Championship. For example, Denmark would never have won the 1992 crown without Schmeichel, whose intimidating presence between the posts forced Marco Van Basten into missing the decisive kick in the penalty shoot-out which climaxed the semi-final against Holland. Schmeichel began the career which turned into his country's best-ever goalkeeper with the part-timers of Hvidovre, moved up to Brondby — where the Laudrup brothers, Brian and Michael, started — then joined Manchester United for what is now clearly a bargain £800,000. He proved a linchpin of their championship-dominating side of the mid-1990s. Before joining United, he worked part-time running a charity shop for the World Wildlife Fund and then in the advertisement department of a local newspaper. Now *he* makes the headlines.

Denmark

David Seaman

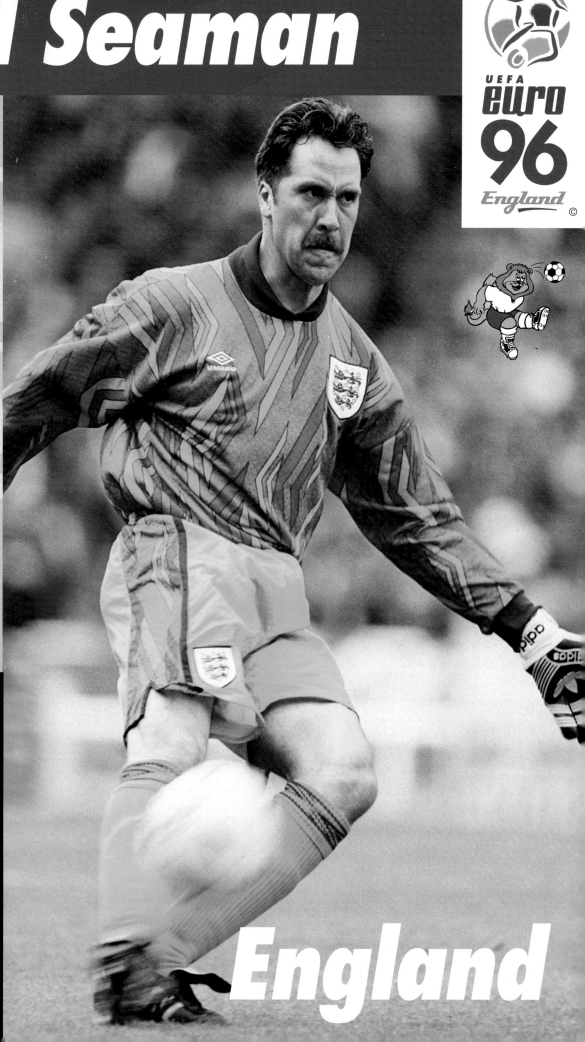

The giant hands of David Seaman provide the insurance policy for England's assault on EURO 96™. He certainly knows all about the ups and downs of top-level international football. In May 1994, Seaman was a Cup-winners Cup hero as Arsenal defeated Parma in Copenhagen to win their first European trophy since the 1970 triumph over Belgium's Anderlecht in the old Inter-City Fairs Cup. One year later, Seaman was again in the spotlight, this time defying Sampdoria of Genoa in a semi-final shoot-out in Italy. He could do no wrong. The Final, in Paris, was a different story. Zaragoza's former Spurs midfielder Nayim foxed Seaman with a towering long-range lob in injury time which flew up into the glare of the floodlights around the stadium roof, and dropped down over Seaman's head, just beneath his crossbar. Not that such an incident could faze a player who had fought his way so tenaciously up the football ladder. Seaman began at Leeds United, joined Peterborough United, then Birmingham City, before moving to London with Queens Park Rangers. Arsenal paid what was then a domestic record fee for a goalkeeper of £1.3 million in 1990. In his first season, he collected a championship medal, conceding just 18 goals, then helped secure the 1992–93 double cup triumphs. Seaman had, by then, been an England squad regular since 1988 – emphasizing the experience he brings to his country's EURO 96™ challenge.

BORN: Rotherham, 19 September 1963

CLUBS: Leeds United, Peterborough United, Birmingham City, Queens Park Rangers, Arsenal

POSITION/STYLE OF PLAY: Goalkeeper/big man with remarkable agility

INTERNATIONAL CAREER: Debut vs. Saudi Arabia, 1988 (20 appearances)

MOST LIKELY TO: Save the crucial spot-kick in any penalty shoot-out

LEAST LIKELY TO: Want to face Spanish opposition

England

Alan Shearer

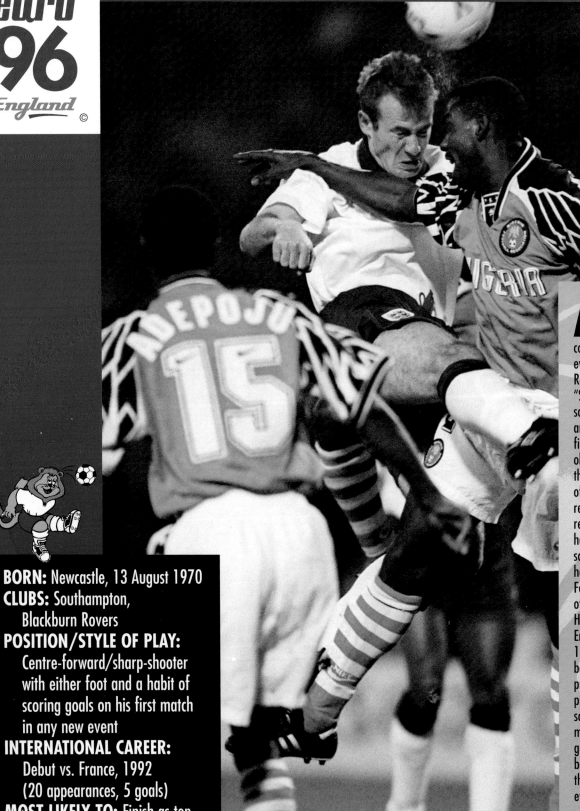

BORN: Newcastle, 13 August 1970

CLUBS: Southampton, Blackburn Rovers

POSITION/STYLE OF PLAY: Centre-forward/sharp-shooter with either foot and a habit of scoring goals on his first match in any new event

INTERNATIONAL CAREER: Debut vs. France, 1992 (20 appearances, 5 goals)

MOST LIKELY TO: Finish as top scorer at EURO 96™

LEAST LIKELY TO: End EURO 96™ without a goal to his name

Alan Shearer is the man the rest of Europe fear as they prepare to take on England at EURO 96™. National coach Terry Venables once summed up what every opponent feels about Blackburn Rovers' centre-forward when he said: "Shearer is so good it's frightening. He can score goals with his head, with his right foot and with his left foot. When it comes to finishing, his strength is that he's got no obvious weaknesses." It was England's loss that a serious knee injury ruled Shearer out of the 1992 European finals. But he recovered and was soon justifying the then record £3.6 million fee which Blackburn had paid Southampton for him. Shearer scored on his England debut against France, has been top league marksman as well as Footballer of the Year, and has been talked of as a "new Geoff Hurst". The old West Ham hero, of course, scored a hat-trick in England's victory over West Germany in the 1966 World Cup Final. But Shearer has been marked out for stardom ever since his primary school days. His goalscoring prowess was already such that he once scored 13 of his team's 17 goals before the match was abandoned. Naturally, he graduated to a trial with Newcastle. But, because he also tried out as a goalkeeper, they did not sign him. Their loss has been everyone else's gain.

England

Tomas Skuhravy

Tomas Skuhravy once claimed he would have been happier driving a high-speed, high-horse-powered Ferrari around a grand prix circuit than playing in a major football event. But, for all the temptations which may have been in evidence during his six years as a professional in Italy, the home of Ferrari, Skuhravy has remained faithful to football. It was, in fact, at the 1990 World Cup finals in Italy where he earned worldwide fame with his marksmanship exploits. Skuhravy scored a hat-trick in Czechoslovakia's 6–1 defeat of the United States, and finished the tournament as five-goal, second-top scorer overall, behind Toto Schillaci. He was rewarded for his brilliance with an instant transfer from Sparta Prague to Genoa. His attacking partnership with Uruguay's Carlos Aguilera brought Genoa their highest placing for years in the league and entry into the UEFA Cup, where they reached the semi-finals. Thereafter it went downhill for Genoa, with only Skuhravy's goals standing between them and relegation. Following the inevitable drop, in 1995, Skuhravy had a short, unhappy spell with Sporting Lisbon of Portugal. At international level, however, Skuhravy has taken Czechoslovakia's conversion into the Czech Republic in his goalscoring stride. All his "new" country now asks is that he emulates the form he showed at the highest level in the "old days".

BORN: Ceske Budejovice, 7 September 1965
CLUBS: Sparta Prague, Genoa (Italy), Sporting Lisbon (Portugal), Genoa
POSITION/STYLE OF PLAY: Centre-forward/ tall but dangerous not only in the air but on the ground and especially at corners and free kicks
INTERNATIONAL CAREER: Czechoslovakia debut vs. Poland, 1985; Czech Republic debut vs. Lithuania, 1994 (49 appearances, 17 goals)
MOST LIKELY TO: Give his marker vertigo
LEAST LIKELY TO: Drive a Fiat Uno

Czech Rep.

Paulo Sousa

Paulo Sousa has been the most outstanding of the recent wave of Portuguese imports into Italian football. He made his name with Benfica, for whom he played almost 150 league, cup and European games, before being sold to Juventus in the summer of 1994. Now he offers the midfield anchor for a Portuguese side who could prove one of the most exciting of the European Championship finals. As Marcello Lippi, coach of the Juventus team whom Sousa helped win the 1995 Italian league title, says: "Paulo is the classical deep-lying general. He is as important to his team in breaking down attacks as he is in organizing his team-mates." At school he was bright and a teacher's favourite. He even considered training to become a teacher himself. But Sousa's football ability was even stronger competition. Sousa scored a hatful of goals for local youth team Repesesc, and Portugal's top clubs came calling, offering all sorts of riches, far beyond anything attainable by teaching. In the end it was no contest, and Benfica won the arguments for his signature. Incredibly, Repesesc collected a mere £400 transfer fee. Carlos Queiroz, the national technical director, called up Sousa for the Portuguese junior squad. He helped win the 1989 World Youth Cup in Saudi Arabia and returned home a teenage hero. Who knows what sort of heroics he may produce at EURO 96™?

BORN: Viseu, 30 August 1970
CLUBS: Repesesc, Benfica, Sporting Clube, Juventus (Italy)
POSITION/STYLE OF PLAY: Midfielder/likes to sit just behind the other midfielders, breaking up opposing attacks as well as setting up his own
INTERNATIONAL CAREER: Debut vs. Holland, 1992 (22 appearances)
MOST LIKELY TO: Be hailed as good an export as Madeira
LEAST LIKELY TO: Go back to teaching – unless it's football

Portugal

Hristo Stoichkov

Hristo Stoichkov has absolutely no doubt about his ability, nor his status as one of the world's leading footballers. No other player would have dared boast, as he did in 1995, that Barcelona had sold him to Parma: "because Johan Cruyff was jealous of my achievements and the fans' love for me." Dutchman Cruyff, whose achievements place him among the all-time greats, was able to laugh off the Bulgarian's bravado. But plenty of other teams and players have had to admit to Stoichkov's superior talents. It was, in fact, on Cruyff's personal recommendation that Barcelona made Stoichkov the most expensive Bulgarian footballer to that time, by paying CSKA Sredets £2 million for him in 1990. Stoichkov had already been an international regular for two years, and Barcelona were quickest off the mark to take advantage of the collapse of Bulgaria's barrier on foreign transfers. Barcelona's fans were initially doubtful about Cruyff's choice, but soon changed their minds. Stoichkov was four times a Spanish league championship winner with Barcelona, once Bulgarian Sportsman of the Year and then winner of the European Footballer of the Year prize in 1994. He won the European Champions Cup against Sampdoria at Wembley in 1992, and inspired Bulgaria's best-ever World Cup to fourth place at USA '94. Now he believes another European title is just around the corner – back in England.

BORN: Sofia, 8 February 1966

CLUBS: CSKA Sofia, Barcelona (Spain), Parma (Italy)

POSITION/STYLE OF PLAY: Forward/angular runner but deceptively quick, likes to switch between attack leader and the spaces wide on the wings

INTERNATIONAL CAREER: Debut vs. Belgium, 1987 (59 appearances, 29 goals)

MOST LIKELY TO: Wear a sponsor's cap for TV interviews

LEAST LIKELY TO: Congratulate the referee on a good game

Bulgaria

Davor Suker

Davor Suker shares a passion with actress Liz Hurley – for Versace clothes. Croatia's centre-forward is not merely their leader in terms of fashion, though. Suker is their top scorer – with 16 goals in 15 internationals – their domestic Footballer of the Year for the past three seasons, and the key negotiator when it comes to sitting down with federation officials and sponsors and talking about pay and bonuses. Whatever may happen at EURO 96™, Suker will be able to indulge his fashion tastes in an even more extravagant manner thanks to the lucrative contract he is about to take up with Spanish giants Real Madrid. Suker's marksmanship for his country – he was top overall scorer in the European Championship qualifying competition with 12 goals in 10 games – ensured that struggling Spanish club Sevilla would be unable to hold onto him. Germany's big-spending Bayern Munich wanted Suker but, in the end, it was Suker's love of his adopted homeland of Spain which helped Madrid win the day. When it comes to EURO 96™, Suker is confident Croatia will do well. As he points out, no fewer than 11 members of Croatia's likely squad of 22 grew up with Dinamo – now FC Croatia – of Zagreb, including himself and midfield superstars Zvonimir Boban and Robert Prosinecki. Having shared, nine years ago, in the former Yugoslavia's World Youth Cup success, they want a repeat which would mean so much more.

BORN: Osijek, 1 January 1968

CLUBS: Osijek, Dinamo Zagreb, Sevilla (Spain)

POSITION/STYLE OF PLAY: Centre-forward/ dynamic attacking leader who has the accelerating advantage over just about every central defender

INTERNATIONAL CAREER: Debut vs. Romania, 1990 (15 appearances, 16 goals)

MOST LIKELY TO: Splash out on fashionwear more than sportswear

LEAST LIKELY TO: Worry about safety pins

Croatia

Gianfranco Zola

BORN: Oliena, 5 July 1966
CLUBS: Nuorese, Torres, Napoli, Parma
POSITION/STYLE OF PLAY:
Midfield/can sit back in the depths of midfield or tuck in behind the strikers when Italy are on the attack
INTERNATIONAL CAREER:
Debut vs. Norway, 1991 (18 appearances, 7 goals)
MOST LIKELY TO:
Score from a direct free kick just outside the penalty box
LEAST LIKELY TO:
Write like his French namesake, Emile

Italy

Italy has always enjoyed the services of highly-gifted attackers. From Giuseppe Meazza and Silvio Piola in the 1930s, to Gianni Rivera, Sandro Mazzola and Luigi Riva in the 1960s and 1970s and, more recently, Paolo Rossi, Gianluca Vialli and Roberto Baggio. All have played their football for the fashionable giants such as Milan, Juventus and Internazionale. That's where Italy's new hero, Gianfranco Zola, is different. He too brings to the Italian national team midfield craft and an eye for goal, but he does so from the springboard of provincial Parma – the surprise package of the 1990s. Zola began as a support striker with his local club Nuorese in the fourth division, then moved to rivals Torres, before being picked up by Napoli in 1989. His technical ability and mop of hair made comparisons with Diego Maradona inevitable, especially when Zola made his debut as the Argentine's deputy. He came into his own after Maradona's hasty departure for Argentina, and developed a lethal talent with free kicks from anywhere around the penalty box. Italian statisticians have worked out that Zola's goal strike-rate from direct free kicks is superior even to that of former France and Juventus superstar Michel Platini. When Arrigo Sacchi picks his squad for EURO 96™, Zola will be one of the first names inked in – ahead of the likes of even Roberto Baggio and Co.

Andoni Zubizarreta

BORN: Vitoria, 23 October 1961
CLUBS: Athletic Bilbao, Barcelona,
   Valencia
POSITION/STYLE PLAY:
   Goalkeeper/secure hands, loud
   voice to direct defensive operations
   among his team-mates
INTERNATIONAL CAREER:
   Debut vs. Finland, 1985
   (105 appearances)
MOST LIKELY TO:
   Keep on playing until he is 40
LEAST LIKELY TO:
   Do Holland any favours

Spain

The day before Spain play an international, coach Javier Clemente tells just one man what his team line-up will be: goalkeeper-captain Andoni Zubizarreta. The rest of the squad – as well as the fans and the opposition – all have to wait until shortly before kick-off to find out who is playing. Such trust reflects the respect which Clemente bears the first Spanish player to top a century of international appearances. "Zubi" has long been acknowledged as one of Europe's finest goalkeepers. A product of the remarkable Basque school of goalkeeping, he was discovered by Athletic Bilbao in 1981, and thrown in at the first division deep end by then manager Ronnie Allen. Zubizarreta helped Bilbao win the league in 1982 and the league-and-cup double a year later, before joining Barcelona in 1986 for a then world goalkeeping record of £1.2 million. The climax of his club career was when he led the Catalan giants to their 1992 Champions Cup Final victory over Italy's Sampdoria at Wembley. Two years later, in Athens, however, Barcelona coach Johan Cruyff blamed Zubizarreta – unfairly most critics felt – for their 4–0 defeat in the Final by Milan, and gave him a free transfer. Valencia president Francisco Roig believed Zubizarreta still had plenty to offer, and his form has continued to go from strength to strength. Javier Clemente is clearly of the same opinion.